Book of House Design for Minecraft

Everything you need to know about what it takes to create beautiful homes in Minecraft!

Acquire Complete **ULTIMATE** Book Collection!

Minecraft: Ultimate Book of Secrets

Minecraft: Ultimate Building Book

Minecraft: Ultimate Building Ideas

Minecraft: Ultimate Redstone Book

Master Minecraft Together With Us!

Minecraft: Ultimate Book of Traps

Minecraft: Ultimate Survival Book

Minecraft: Ultimate Book of Battle

Minecraft: Ultimate Book of Seeds

Explore Our Marvelous Minecraft Novels

Defender of The Ender

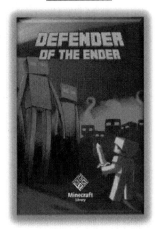

In Search of Herobrine

Incredible Tale Of Steve

Licence Notes

Table of Contents

Introduction

Just like in the real world, it is extremely important to have a house in Minecraft! Your house should be used as your primary location for all the important parts in Minecraft, whether it be Storage, Smelting, Crafting or Brewing! You can place your spawn point inside a house, by sleeping in a bed!

Since you will be using your house very frequently, it is valuable to make it pleasing to you. This guide will show you some ideas you can use to create the best house possible!

Exterior Designs

This section of the guide will present you with a wide range of different houses that can be built in Minecraft. Some of these houses a gigantic mansions that can take weeks to build, while others are small and cozy cottages that can be constructed in a few minutes! During this section, we will only discuss exterior designing. Interior decorations will be presented next!

Living like a King

  While it is cool to build a small, simplistic castle and call it a day, nothing beats having a huge, highly detailed design like this! This castle would take days, if not weeks, to design and construct! Many different materials are used in this design, but a unique design element used is the blending of ice and fire!

The Modern

This style of housing has become very popular in the Minecraft world! It is common to build the exterior with quartz blocks or white wool, to give off a clean, sleek appearance. Use floor to ceiling windows, and lots of balconies to complete this design!

Plain ol' House

This is the most basic, yet functional, style of house in Minecraft. It can be built with most materials, but wood is primarily used because it is easy to obtain! This house is perfect for new players, or players looking for a temporary shelter!

Plain ol' House Plus

Like the previous design, this house relies on simplicity and ease of construction. However, this specific design features a bonus porch, which could be used as a great place for a horse!

Cabin in the Woods

This design is perfect for anybody who loves the forest! It can be made using logs, planks and cobblestone, so it is ideal for new players! Unlike the previous designs, this house features some more interesting aesthetics, such as the overhanging roof or the chimney!

Farmer's Delight!

Farming can be a very important part of your Minecraft experience, so it may be beneficial to have your house right beside your crops! This design features two floors, a porch, and some enriching details, such as the trapdoors around the windows!

Victorian Style Living!

This house looks shares a lot of visual features as a castle! This is because the design is based off what houses looked like in the Victorian Era. Featuring 2 floors and a basement, as well as a large porch and spruce trim, this house is perfect for all fans of the Victorian Style!

Simple Castle

When are castles not cool?! This design takes all the key elements of a traditional castle, such as a moat, drawbridge, and towers, and wraps it up in an easy and affordable design! Cobblestone is the key building material used, to give that crumbly stone effect.

South western Mansion

Castles are not for everybody, but some people still want to have a huge place to live! A mansion could be a great alternative. This design features large pillars to support the front patio, as well as stone slab trim throughout. This design can be modified in so many ways to fit all your needs!

Chinese Lifestyle!

This design takes cues from ancient traditional Chinese architecture. It can be built with many floors, but each floor must be a bit smaller than the one before to get this specific effect. Red and yellow can be used in the interior, and cobblestone and oak planks for the exterior!

Artic Housing

Igloos can be an amazing addition in any Tundra biome! These houses look amazing, and feel very genuine and natural when done properly. Use an iron door to complete the effect, and to keep mobs out!

Made for Minecraft

There's no argument; pyramids are the easiest and most authentic structures you can build in Minecraft. The use of sandstone blocks in a desert makes this house look and feel as if it came right out of Egypt! Lapis blocks can be used as a decoration inside, because it contrasts nicely with the sandstone!

Living with Friends!

If you are playing on a multiplayer server, it may be very practical and enjoyable to construct condominium housing for you and your friends! These buildings can house as many players as you like, and they look great! Make sure each room has a balcony, and that there is easy access for all the residents!

Living with Friends 2

If you lack the space needed for condos, but have lots of people you need to house, apartments can be a great solution! Just like condos, apartment buildings can be built to house as many players as needed. Wool and glass are commonly used in these designs!

North American Heritage

A Teepee is a traditional shelter invented by the Native Americans. It can be created in Minecraft, offering a very unique and beautiful house! Use wool for this design, and logs for the top!

Useful Rooms!

All houses need rooms in order to be useful! Imagine living in a beautiful house, but with nothing inside! This section of the guide will show you some ideas for different rooms you could add to your house!

Kitchen

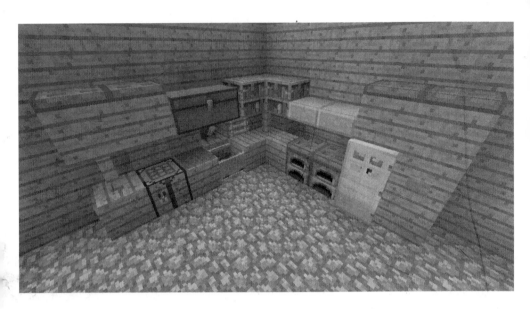

A kitchen is a fun way to incorporate some utilities into your house! Furnaces can be used as ovens, chests as pantries, and cauldrons as sinks! Kitchens could also be a great place to set up brewing stations or smelting rooms!

Bedroom

It's no fun to respawn in a barren wasteland when you die, so creating a bedroom could be a great addition to your spawn point! Sleeping in a bed sets your spawn point, then decorate your room with some bookshelves and lights!

Living Room

A living room is always a positive addition to any house because it is a place for you to relax after a long day of mining! Living rooms can be modeled in so many styles to fit your preferences, and are also a great room to meet with guests!

Library

Most houses in Minecraft have an enchanting table, so why not develop the bookshelves into a full library? Libraries can be built extremely big, or just as a small study room. It also shows guests that you like to read!

Storage Room

It is very important to have all your belongings sorted in specific chests, and a storage room is a great place to keep these chests! Use item frames to represent the contents of different chests, and always keep a few crafting tables and ender chests handy!

Dining Room

When you are starving and need a bite to eat, just head over to your dining room! This is a great spot for your guests to have a meeting as well.

Interior Design!

What's a house without some furnishing? Like all homes, it is important to have a beautiful interior that compliments what you see from outside. This section of the guide will show you different things you can do to improve your house!

Seating!

There are very many designs on how to create the best chair in Minecraft, but the best one by most people's standards is the simple stair and sign combo! These seats can be placed anywhere around your house!

Tables

There are many different methods to creating realistic looking tables for your house. One common method is using activated pistons facing upwards! Fences and carpet can also be used together to create great tables

Refrigerator

This could be a great addition to your kitchen! Fill the dispenser with food, so when you press the button, food will launch out!

Staircases

Many people decide to just use ladders to travel to different floors, but it looks much better to add staircases! There are many different styles, from spiral staircases to ramp styles!

Chandeliers

If you have a castle or mansion style house, and have a large, open space that needs a little something "extra", you should consider adding a chandelier! Torches or glowstone can be used as the actual lighting mechanism, and fences can be used as the supports.

Sofas

Sofas can be great additions to living rooms, foyers, or even bedrooms! They can be created using wool and upside-down steps, and can be as big or small as you need!

Television

    While not the most practical or useful decoration for your house, a TV could be added just as a fun little memento from the real world! Adding a large painting to the front can make it look as if it was really on!

Fireplace

Not only does it look good, but a fireplace can also be a great source of lighting for your house! Put down Netherrack where you want the fire to be, and set it on fire! Make sure there is no wood or wool close by, or your house may burn down!

Flowers Inside!

Use flower pots to hold your favorite flower! Place them all over your house as a little bit of extra colour!

Paintings

Paintings are a great way to brighten up your house! They can be put up just about anywhere and can really brighten up a room!

Guides

This is the final chapter of this book, where you will be given a few guides on how to create lots of different aspects of a house!

Fireplace #1

Start off with 2 pieces of Netherrack. These blocks will burn forever once lit, so they make for great firewood!

Fireplace #2

Place whatever block you want around the netherrack. This block should go with the rest of the material used in your house.

Fireplace #3

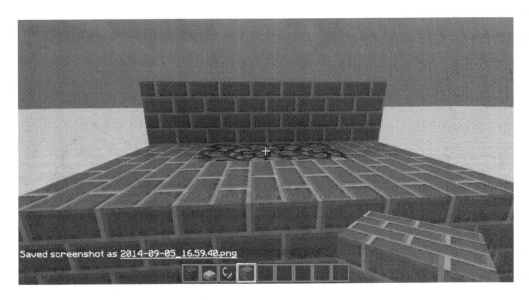

Saved screenshot as 2014-09-05_16.59.40.png

Build 1 block higher on the side that will be against the wall. Skip this step if your fireplace will be in the middle of the room.

Fireplace #4

Light the netherrack with flint and steel, then place glass blocks on top of the blocks you chose.

Fireplace #5

Above the flames, build a 2x2 chimney as tall as you want. This step can also be skipped if you like.

Fireplace #6

Place 1 more set of blocks above the glass, and you have your very own fireplace!

Piston Table #1

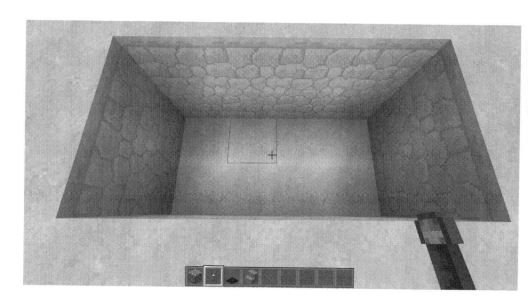

Dig a 2 block deep hole in the ground, and make is 2x8 blocks in width and length.

Piston Table #3

Place redstone torches at the bottom of the
hole. These will activate the pistons.

Piston Table #3

Place the pistons, facing upwards, on each of the torches. They will activate and push up.

Piston Table #4

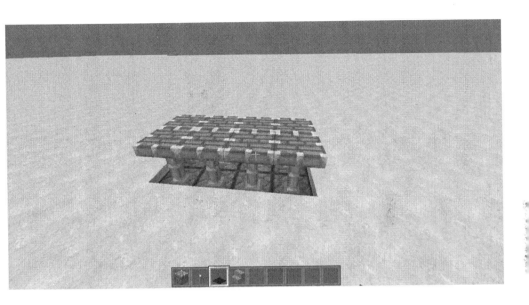

This should be what you have so far.

Piston Table #5

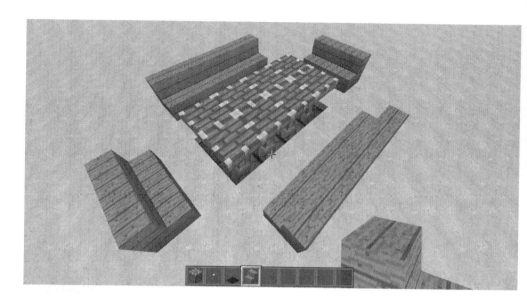

Place stair blocks around the pistons, 1 block back. These will be the chairs for the table.

Piston Table #6

Choose any type of carpet and place it on top of the pistons. This will make it look like the table has a cloth on it.

Piston Table #7

Tidy up the floor and you have a great looking table and chairs!

Small House #1

Start with a 4 block high beam. Logs are usually a great choice.

Small House #2

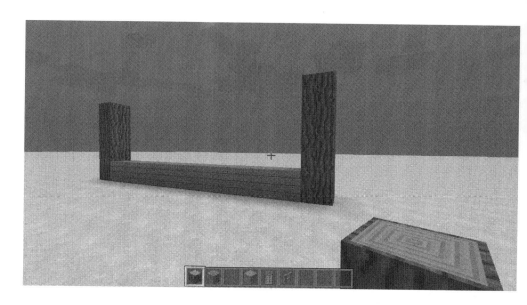

Create a 1 block high row and end it with another beam. It needs to be and odd number of blocks!

Small House #3

The pattern goes wood, glass, wood, glass. Start with wood, and continue the pattern the whole way down.

Small House #4

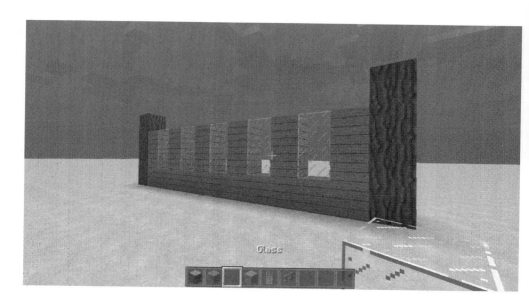

Depending on how long you decided to make the wall, it should look something like this.

Small House #5

Place another row of whatever block you want over the glass.

Small House #6

Follow the same steps for the next side wall. This wall should be a bit shorter than the previous.

Small House #7

Make an identical wall on the other side as well.

Small House #8

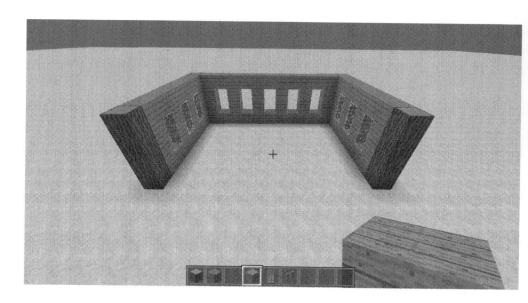

You should have a frame somewhat like this.

Small House #9

This step is subjective to how wide you made the frame, but you should be able to make a frame around a door, with another row of blocks on either side.

Small House #10

Windows on the front should be squares.
Make one on either side of the door!

Small House #11

Finish off the front with another layer to clean everything up!

Small House #12

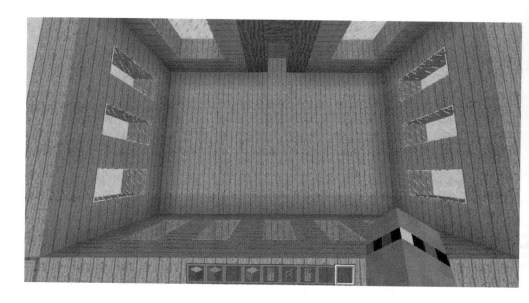

Place down a floor with whatever block you think will look nice.

Small House #13

For the roof, make 1 row on top of what you have already.

Small House #14

Cover it all up!

Small House #15

Make sure to have lighting and you are done!

Storage Room #1

Start by making a 5 block high pillar. It needs to be 2 blocks deep.

Storage Room #2

Place another pillar 1 block away, and then another one between the two, 2 blocks back.

Storage Room #3

Repeat this until you are happy with the number of columns you have.

Storage Room #4

Place 4 double chests in each column!

Storage Room #5

Place glowstone on top of the chests. Unlike regular blocks, you can open a chest even if there is a block of glowstone above it!

Storage Room #6

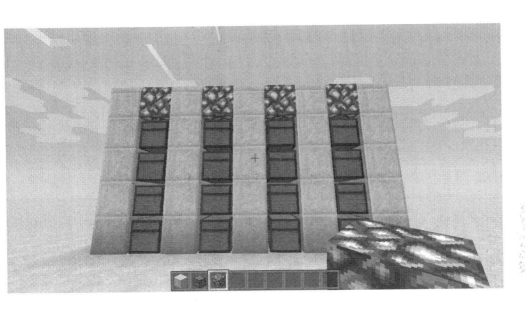

This is what your first wall should look like!

Storage Room #7

It helps to add item frames to the chest, with a symbol of each content inside!

Storage Room #8

Finish the other 2 walls using the same design!

Storage Room #9

Make your roof 1 block higher than the glowstone, so you can use it as a light source as well!

Storage Room #10

Don't forget to add your utilities as well!

Curving Staircase #1

Start with a 4x3 hollow wall, with 4 quartz slabs to either side.

Curving Staircase #2

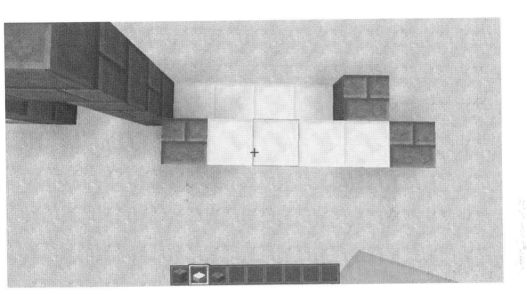

    For the next row of quartz slabs, shift it over by one block, and raise it by half a block as well.

Curving Staircase #3

Raise the stone blocks up each time the quartz slabs are the same height.

Curving Staircase #4

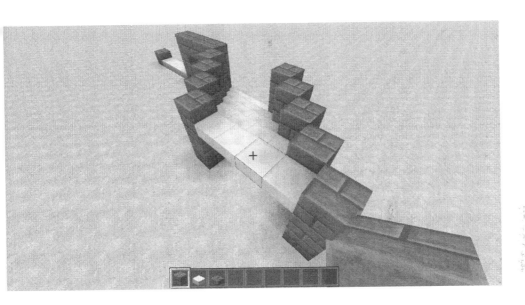

Once the stone blocks are the same height as the 4x3 hallow wall, stop raising them.

Curving Staircase #5

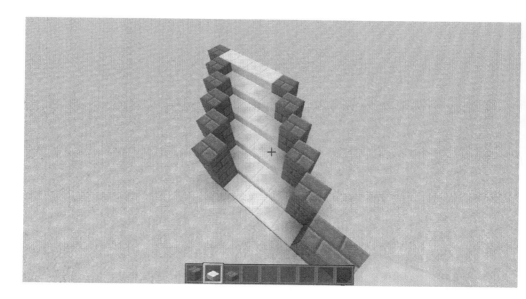

This is what the first side should look like.

Curving Staircase #6

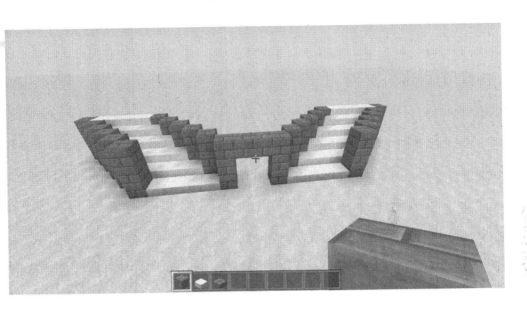

Repeat steps 2 – 5 on the other side!

Curving Staircase #7

Connet the 2 sides to each other, and place a row of stone on the inside as well.

Curving Staircase #8

You can now use this staircase however you want! The middle is also a great place for a fountain!

39006742R00054

Made in the USA
Lexington, KY
03 February 2015